Welcome to your new gratitude journal!

We are so grateful you chose this journal and would like to make your experience even better than you expected!

Here is our gift to you

D1368117

Freebies for You!

1. FREE Gratitude Course
2. FREE videos on how gratitude changes lives
3. Scientific benefits of gratitude and surprise freebies

VISIT OUR WEBSITE

https://www.HowtoLearn.com/Free-Gratitude-Course

Discover more of our books here:

https://www.amazon.com/author/patwyman

Thank You for Leaving a Book Review Online.

If you enjoy this book, thank you for leaving a book review online. People benefit from your review and we always love hearing what you like and what we can do better!

How to Use This Journal

This is a 52-week guide to living a happier, more fulfilled life! You can record your moment of gratitude each day, and see a full week at a glance.

If you want to make your gratitude deeper and more meaningful so that it has a lasting impact all day long, jot down what you are grateful for and the reasons you feel thankful. Studies show that writing what are grateful for at the beginning of your day positively affects the entire day Journal your gratitude at night and you go to sleep with a peaceful, happy heart. So, if you like, it feels great to do both!

BONUS: If you love to relax and color, use the designs at the top of each page!

SCIENCE-BACKED BENEFITS OF GRATITUDE

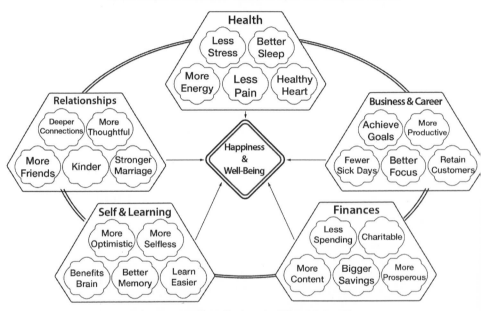

Data: More than 26 studies from the NIH and Universities.
Courtesy of Pat Wyman, Author
The One-Minute Gratitude Journal: For the Moments That Matter

Inquiries for the publisher or to purchase One Minute Journals in bulk:
oneminutejournals@gmail.com

ISBN Paperback: 978-1-890047-65-8   Digital Book: 978-1-890047-49-8
10 9 8 7 6 5 4 3 2   1st Edition, December 2018

Can you Transform Your Life in One Minute a Day? How Will It Be Better When You Do?

Gratitude journaling makes it easy. Studies show that by focusing on gratitude you can improve mental and physical health, have better relationships, be more determined to achieve your goals, reduce pain and anxiety and even sleep better!

The simple act of writing down what you are grateful for, as you begin and end each day, allows you to become purpose-driven and find many more minutes that matter in your life.

As you write in your new gratitude journal, think of things each day you are grateful for. They can be as simple as you watched a sunset, had a good night's sleep, enjoyed your morning coffee, or received praise from a friend or family member.

When you head out on your morning commute, find one thing to be grateful for. During your work day, look for any new inspiration and other reasons to be thankful. If you have kids, catch them being good and tell them! The whole family will be grateful.

Finally, every evening, ask yourself this question: "What was the best thing that happened today?"

The *One-Minute Gratitude Journal* helps you live each day with a grateful, happy heart and in the minutes you write, you'll build new habits that increase your overall well-being and balance in life. You will create a beautiful attitude of gratitude and find yourself feeling more content and happier every day.

Yes, you can change your life in just one minute a day. Turn your ordinary moments into blessings.

This is a wonderful day.
I've never seen this one before.

MAYA ANGELOU

Today I am *Grateful* for: DATE :_____

_____

_____

_____

_____

Today I am *Grateful* for: DATE :_____

_____

_____

_____

_____

Friends and Family I am Grateful For

DATE :_____

_____

_____

_____

Gratitude is a powerful catalyst for happiness.
It's the spark that lights a fire of joy in your soul.

AMY COLLETTE

Today I am *Grateful* for: DATE :_____

_____

_____

Today I am *Grateful* for: DATE :_____

_____

_____

Today I am *Grateful* for: DATE :_____

_____

_____

Moments that Made Me Smile

DATE :_____

_____

_____

_____

Many times a day I realize how much my own life is built on the labors of my fellowmen, and how earnestly I must exert myself in order to give in return as much as I have received.

ALBERT EINSTEIN

Today I am *Grateful* for:

DATE :_____

_____

_____

_____

_____

Today I am *Grateful* for:

DATE :_____

_____

_____

_____

_____

Things I Did for Myself that Made Me Happy

DATE :_____

_____

_____

_____

When it comes to life the critical thing is whether you take things for granted or take them with gratitude.

G.K. CHESTERTON

Today I am *Grateful* for: DATE :_____

_____

_____

Today I am *Grateful* for: DATE :_____

_____

_____

Today I am *Grateful* for: DATE :_____

_____

_____

Random Acts of Kindness I Did or Someone Did for Me

DATE :_____

_____

_____

_____

Thankfulness is an attitude of possibilities, not an attitude of liabilities.

CRAIG D. LOUNSBROUGH

Today I am *Grateful* for: DATE :_____

_____

_____

_____

_____

Today I am *Grateful* for: DATE :_____

_____

_____

_____

_____

Before Sleep Each Night Ask Yourself,
"What Is the Best Thing That Happened Today?"

DATE :_____

_____

_____

_____

Let gratitude be the pillow upon which you kneel to say your nightly prayer. And let faith be the bridge you build to overcome evil and welcome good.

MAYA ANGELOU

Today I am *Grateful* for: DATE :_____

_____

_____

Today I am *Grateful* for: DATE :_____

_____

_____

Today I am *Grateful* for: DATE :_____

_____

_____

Friends and Family I am Grateful For

DATE :_____

_____

_____

_____

Gratitude is the fairest blossom which springs from the soul.

HENRY WARD BEECHER

Today I am *Grateful* for: DATE :_____

_____

_____

_____

_____

Today I am *Grateful* for: DATE :_____

_____

_____

_____

_____

Moments that Made Me Smile

DATE :_____

_____

_____

_____

Happiness cannot be traveled to, owned, earned, worn or consumed. Happiness is the spiritual experience of living every minute with love, grace, and gratitude.

DENIS WAITLEY

Today I am *Grateful* for: DATE :_____

_____

_____

Today I am *Grateful* for: DATE :_____

_____

_____

Today I am *Grateful* for: DATE :_____

_____

_____

Things I Did for Myself that Made Me Happy

DATE :_____

_____

_____

_____

Gratitude is when memory is stored in the heart and not in the mind.

LIONEL HAMPTON

Today I am *Grateful* for: DATE :_____

_____

_____

_____

_____

Today I am *Grateful* for: DATE :_____

_____

_____

_____

_____

Random Acts of Kindness I Did or Someone Did for Me

DATE :_____

_____

_____

_____

Gratitude is not only the greatest of virtues but the parent of all others.

MARCUS TULLIUS CICERO

Today I am *Grateful* for: DATE :_____

_____

_____

Today I am *Grateful* for: DATE :_____

_____

_____

Today I am *Grateful* for: DATE :_____

_____

_____

Before Sleep Each Night Ask Yourself,
"What Is the Best Thing That Happened Today?"

DATE :_____

_____

_____

_____

I would maintain that thanks are the highest form of thought, and that gratitude is happiness doubled by wonder.

GILBERT C. CHESTERTON

Today I am *Grateful* for:
DATE :_____

_____

_____

_____

_____

Today I am *Grateful* for:
DATE :_____

_____

_____

_____

_____

Friends and Family I am Grateful For

DATE :_____

_____

_____

_____

As we express our gratitude, we must never forget that the highest appreciation is not to utter words, but to live by them.

JOHN F. KENNEDY

Today I am *Grateful* for: DATE :_____

_____

_____

Today I am *Grateful* for: DATE :_____

_____

_____

Today I am *Grateful* for: DATE :_____

_____

_____

Moments that Made Me Smile

DATE :_____

_____

_____

_____

When I started counting my blessings,
my whole life turned around.

WILLIE NELSON

Today I am *Grateful* for: DATE :_____

_____

_____

_____

_____

Today I am *Grateful* for: DATE :_____

_____

_____

_____

_____

Things I Did for Myself that Made Me Happy

DATE :_____

_____

_____

_____

has been said that life has treated me harshly; and sometimes I have complained
my heart because many pleasures of human experience have been withheld from
me ... if much has been denied me, much, very much, has been given me....

HELEN KELLER

Today I am *Grateful* for: DATE :_____

_____

_____

Today I am *Grateful* for: DATE :_____

_____

_____

Today I am *Grateful* for: DATE :_____

_____

_____

Random Acts of Kindness I Did or Someone Did for Me

DATE :_____

_____

_____

_____

The more grateful I am, the more beauty I see.

MARY DAVIS

Today I am *Grateful* for: DATE :_____

_____

_____

_____

_____

Today I am *Grateful* for: DATE :_____

_____

_____

_____

_____

Before Sleep Each Night Ask Yourself,
"What Is the Best Thing That Happened Today?"

DATE :_____

_____

_____

_____

The invariable mark of wisdom is to see the miraculous in the common.

RALPH WALDO EMERSON

Today I am *Grateful* for: DATE :_____

_____

_____

Today I am *Grateful* for: DATE :_____

_____

_____

Today I am *Grateful* for: DATE :_____

_____

_____

Friends and Family I am Grateful For

DATE :_____

_____

_____

_____

Gratitude unlocks the fullness of life.
It turns what we have into enough, and more...

MELODY BEATTIE

Today I am *Grateful* for: DATE :_____

_____

_____

_____

_____

Today I am *Grateful* for: DATE :_____

_____

_____

_____

_____

Moments that Made Me Smile

DATE :_____

_____

_____

_____

Today I choose to live with gratitude for the love that fills my heart, the peace that rests within my spirit, and the voice of hope that says all things are possible.

ANONYMOUS

Today I am *Grateful* for: DATE :_____

_____

_____

Today I am *Grateful* for: DATE :_____

_____

_____

Today I am *Grateful* for: DATE :_____

_____

_____

Things I Did for Myself that Made Me Happy

DATE :_____

_____

_____

_____

Every time we remember to say "thank you",
we experience nothing less than heaven on earth.

SARAH BAN BREATHNACH

Today I am *Grateful* for:

DATE :_____

_____

_____

_____

_____

Today I am *Grateful* for:

DATE :_____

_____

_____

_____

_____

Random Acts of Kindness I Did or Someone Did for Me

DATE :_____

_____

_____

_____

My gratitude for good writing is unbounded;
I'm grateful for it the way I'm grateful for the ocean.

ANNE LAMOTT

Today I am *Grateful* for: DATE :_____

_____

_____

Today I am *Grateful* for: DATE :_____

_____

_____

Today I am *Grateful* for: DATE :_____

_____

_____

Before Sleep Each Night Ask Yourself,
"What Is the Best Thing That Happened Today?"

DATE :_____

_____

_____

_____

Gratitude is the sign of noble souls.

A E S O P

Today I am *Grateful* for: DATE :_____

_____

_____

_____

_____

Today I am *Grateful* for: DATE :_____

_____

_____

_____

_____

Friends and Family I am Grateful For

DATE :_____

_____

_____

_____

Nothing is more honorable than a grateful heart.

LUCIUS ANNAEUS SENECA

oday I am *Grateful* for: DATE :_____

_____

_____

oday I am *Grateful* for: DATE :_____

_____

_____

oday I am *Grateful* for: DATE :_____

_____

_____

Moments that Made Me Smile

DATE :_____

_____

_____

_____

When you are grateful, fear disappears and abundance appears.

ANTHONY ROBBINS

Today I am *Grateful* for: DATE :_____

_____

_____

_____

_____

Today I am *Grateful* for: DATE :_____

_____

_____

_____

_____

Things I Did for Myself that Made Me Happy

DATE :_____

_____

_____

_____

What separates privilege from entitlement is gratitude.

BRENE BROWN

Today I am *Grateful* for: DATE :_____

_____

_____

Today I am *Grateful* for: DATE :_____

_____

_____

Today I am *Grateful* for: DATE :_____

_____

_____

Random Acts of Kindness I Did or Someone Did for Me

DATE :_____

_____

_____

_____

There are only two ways to live your life. One is as though nothing is a miracle. The other is as though everything is a miracle.

ALBERT EINSTEIN

Today I am *Grateful* for: DATE :_____

_____

_____

_____

_____

Today I am *Grateful* for: DATE :_____

_____

_____

_____

_____

Before Sleep Each Night Ask Yourself,
"What Is the Best Thing That Happened Today?"

DATE :_____

_____

_____

_____

No duty is more urgent than that of returning thanks.

JAMES ALLEN

oday I am *Grateful* for: DATE :_____

_____

_____

oday I am *Grateful* for: DATE :_____

_____

_____

oday I am *Grateful* for: DATE :_____

_____

_____

Friends and Family I am Grateful For

DATE :_____

_____

_____

_____

An early-morning walk is a blessing for the whole day.

HENRY DAVID THOREAU

Today I am *Grateful* for: DATE :_____

_____

_____

_____

_____

Today I am *Grateful* for: DATE :_____

_____

_____

_____

_____

Moments that Made Me Smile

DATE :_____

_____

_____

_____

*Today expect something good to happen to you
no matter what occurred yesterday.*

SARAH BAN BREATHNACH

Today I am *Grateful* for: DATE :_____

_____

_____

Today I am *Grateful* for: DATE :_____

_____

_____

Today I am *Grateful* for: DATE :_____

_____

_____

Things I Did for Myself that Made Me Happy

DATE :_____

_____

_____

_____

Our favorite attitude should be gratitude.

ZIG ZIGLAR

Today I am *Grateful* for: DATE :_____

_____

_____

_____

_____

Today I am *Grateful* for: DATE :_____

_____

_____

_____

_____

Random Acts of Kindness I Did or Someone Did for Me

DATE :_____

_____

_____

_____

Better to lose count while naming your blessings than to lose your blessings to counting your troubles.

MALTBIE D. BABCOCK

Today I am *Grateful* for: DATE :_____

_____

_____

Today I am *Grateful* for: DATE :_____

_____

_____

Today I am *Grateful* for: DATE :_____

_____

_____

Before Sleep Each Night Ask Yourself,
"What Is the Best Thing That Happened Today?"

DATE :_____

_____

_____

_____

Gratitude and attitude are not challenges; they are choices.

ROBERT BRAATHE

Today I am *Grateful* for: DATE :_____

_____

_____

_____

_____

Today I am *Grateful* for: DATE :_____

_____

_____

_____

_____

Friends and Family I am Grateful For

DATE :_____

_____

_____

_____

Thanksgiving, after all, is a word of action.

W.J. CAMERON

Today I am *Grateful* for: DATE :_____

_____

_____

Today I am *Grateful* for: DATE :_____

_____

_____

Today I am *Grateful* for: DATE :_____

_____

_____

Moments that Made Me Smile

DATE :_____

_____

_____

_____

To speak gratitude is courteous and pleasant; to enact gratitude is generous and noble, but to live gratitude is to touch heaven.

JOHANNES A. GAERTNER

Today I am *Grateful* for: DATE :_____

_____

_____

_____

_____

Today I am *Grateful* for: DATE :_____

_____

_____

_____

_____

Things I Did for Myself that Made Me Happy

DATE :_____

_____

_____

_____

I am grateful for what I am and have. My thanksgiving is perpetual.

HENRY DAVID THOREAU

oday I am *Grateful* for: DATE :_____

_____

_____

oday I am *Grateful* for: DATE :_____

_____

_____

oday I am *Grateful* for: DATE :_____

_____

_____

Random Acts of Kindness I Did or Someone Did for Me

DATE :_____

_____

_____

_____

You say grace before meals. All right. But I say grace before the concert and the opera, and grace before the play and pantomime, and grace before I open a book, and grace before sketching, painting, swimming, fencing, boxing, walking, playing, dancing and grace before I dip the pen in the ink.

G. K. CHESTERTON

Today I am *Grateful* for:

DATE :_____

_____

_____

_____

_____

Today I am *Grateful* for:

DATE :_____

_____

_____

_____

_____

Before Sleep Each Night Ask Yourself,
"What Is the Best Thing That Happened Today?"

DATE :_____

_____

_____

_____

Not having money to spend doesn't mean we can't have well—spent moments every day.

SARAH BAN BREATHNACH

Today I am *Grateful* for: DATE :_____

_____

_____

Today I am *Grateful* for: DATE :_____

_____

_____

Today I am *Grateful* for: DATE :_____

_____

_____

Friends and Family I am Grateful For

DATE :_____

_____

_____

_____

The thankful receiver bears a plentiful harvest.

WILLIAM BLAKE

Today I am *Grateful* for: DATE :_____

_____

_____

_____

_____

Today I am *Grateful* for: DATE :_____

_____

_____

_____

_____

Moments that Made Me Smile

DATE :_____

_____

_____

_____

We are all messy miracles. Appreciate the mess!

PAT WYMAN

Today I am *Grateful* for:

DATE :_____

_____

_____

Today I am *Grateful* for:

DATE :_____

_____

_____

Today I am *Grateful* for:

DATE :_____

_____

_____

Things I Did for Myself that Made Me Happy

DATE :_____

_____

_____

_____

Train yourself never to put off the word or action for the expression of gratitude.

ALBERT SCHWEITZER

Today I am *Grateful* for: DATE :_____

_____

_____

_____

_____

Today I am *Grateful* for: DATE :_____

_____

_____

_____

_____

Random Acts of Kindness I Did or Someone Did for Me

DATE :_____

_____

_____

_____

My expectations were reduced to zero when I was 21.
Everything since then has been a bonus.

STEPHEN HAWKING

oday I am *Grateful* for: DATE :_____

_____

_____

oday I am *Grateful* for: DATE :_____

_____

_____

oday I am *Grateful* for: DATE :_____

_____

_____

Before Sleep Each Night Ask Yourself,
"What Is the Best Thing That Happened Today?"

DATE :_____

_____

_____

_____

The deepest craving of human nature is the need to be appreciated.

WILLIAM JAMES

Today I am *Grateful* for:　　　　　　　　DATE :_____

_____

_____

_____

_____

Today I am *Grateful* for:　　　　　　　　DATE :_____

_____

_____

_____

_____

Friends and Family I am Grateful For

DATE :_____

_____

_____

_____

So much has been given to me;
I have no time to ponder over that which has been denied.

HELEN KELLER

Today I am *Grateful* for: DATE :_____

_____

_____

Today I am *Grateful* for: DATE :_____

_____

_____

Today I am *Grateful* for: DATE :_____

_____

_____

Moments that Made Me Smile

DATE :_____

_____

_____

_____

At the age of 18, I made up my mind to never have another bad day in my life. I dove into a endless sea of gratitude from which I've never emerged.

PATCH ADAMS

Today I am *Grateful* for: DATE :_____

_____

_____

_____

_____

Today I am *Grateful* for: DATE :_____

_____

_____

_____

_____

Things I Did for Myself that Made Me Happy

DATE :_____

_____

_____

_____

Give your gratitude space to grow, and you will see your whole world change.

ASHLEY REALE

Today I am *Grateful* for: DATE :_____

_____

_____

Today I am *Grateful* for: DATE :_____

_____

_____

Today I am *Grateful* for: DATE :_____

_____

_____

Random Acts of Kindness I Did or Someone Did for Me

DATE :_____

_____

_____

_____

Cultivate the habit of being grateful for every good thing that comes to you, and to give thanks continuously. And because all things have contributed to your advancement, you should include all things in your gratitude.

RALPH WALDO EMERSON

Today I am *Grateful* for: DATE :_____

_____

_____

_____

_____

Today I am *Grateful* for: DATE :_____

_____

_____

_____

_____

Before Sleep Each Night Ask Yourself,
"What Is the Best Thing That Happened Today?"

DATE :_____

_____

_____

_____

To be good, and to do good, is all we have to do.

JOHN ADAMS

Today I am *Grateful* for:　　　　　　　　DATE :_____

_____

_____

Today I am *Grateful* for:　　　　　　　　DATE :_____

_____

_____

Today I am *Grateful* for:　　　　　　　　DATE :_____

_____

_____

Friends and Family I am Grateful For

DATE :_____

_____

_____

_____

*Enjoy the little things, for one day you may look back
and realize they were the big things.*

ROBERT BRAULT

Today I am *Grateful* for: DATE :_____

_____

_____

_____

_____

Today I am *Grateful* for: DATE :_____

_____

_____

_____

_____

Moments that Made Me Smile

DATE :_____

_____

_____

_____

It is not possible to feel grateful and be depressed at the same time.

P A T   W Y M A N

Today I am *Grateful* for: DATE :_____

_____

_____

Today I am *Grateful* for: DATE :_____

_____

_____

Today I am *Grateful* for: DATE :_____

_____

_____

Things I Did for Myself that Made Me Happy

DATE :_____

_____

_____

_____

All which we behold is full of blessings.

WILLIAM WORDSWORTH

Today I am *Grateful* for:
DATE :_____

_____

_____

_____

_____

Today I am *Grateful* for:
DATE :_____

_____

_____

_____

_____

Random Acts of Kindness I Did or Someone Did for Me

DATE :_____

_____

_____

_____

The only people with whom you should try to get even with are those who have helped you.

JOHN E. SOUTHARD

oday I am *Grateful* for:　　　　　　DATE :_____

_____

_____

oday I am *Grateful* for:　　　　　　DATE :_____

_____

_____

oday I am *Grateful* for:　　　　　　DATE :_____

_____

_____

Before Sleep Each Night Ask Yourself,
"What Is the Best Thing That Happened Today?"

DATE :_____

_____

_____

_____

I awoke this morning with devout thanksgiving for my friends, the old and the new.

RALPH WALDO EMERSON

Today I am *Grateful* for:　　　　　　　　DATE :_____

_____

_____

_____

_____

Today I am *Grateful* for:　　　　　　　　DATE :_____

_____

_____

_____

_____

Friends and Family I am Grateful For

DATE :_____

_____

_____

_____

Think with great gratitude of those who have lighted the flame within us.

ALBERT SCHWEITZER

Today I am *Grateful* for: DATE :_____

_____

_____

Today I am *Grateful* for: DATE :_____

_____

_____

Today I am *Grateful* for: DATE :_____

_____

_____

Moments that Made Me Smile

DATE :_____

_____

_____

_____

If you want to turn your life around, try thankfulness.
It will change your life mightily.

GERALD GOOD

Today I am *Grateful* for: DATE :_____

_____

_____

_____

_____

Today I am *Grateful* for: DATE :_____

_____

_____

_____

_____

Things I Did for Myself that Made Me Happy

DATE :_____

_____

_____

_____

What you focus on expands, and when you focus on the goodness in your life, you create more of it. Opportunities, relationships, even money flowed my way when I learned to be grateful no matter what happened in my life.

OPRAH WINFREY

Today I am *Grateful* for: DATE :_____

_____

_____

_____

Today I am *Grateful* for: DATE :_____

_____

_____

_____

Today I am *Grateful* for: DATE :_____

_____

_____

_____

Random Acts of Kindness I Did or Someone Did for Me

DATE :_____

_____

_____

_____

A grateful mind is a great mind which eventually attracts to itself great things.

PLATO

Today I am *Grateful* for: DATE :_____

_____

_____

_____

_____

Today I am *Grateful* for: DATE :_____

_____

_____

_____

_____

Before Sleep Each Night Ask Yourself,
"What Is the Best Thing That Happened Today?"

DATE :_____

_____

_____

_____

Embrace your life journey with gratitude, so that how you travel your path is more important than reaching your ultimate destination.

ROSALENE GLICKMAN

Today I am *Grateful* for: DATE :_____

_____

_____

Today I am *Grateful* for: DATE :_____

_____

_____

Today I am *Grateful* for: DATE :_____

_____

_____

Friends and Family I am Grateful For

DATE :_____

_____

_____

_____

O Lord that lends me life, lend me a heart replete with thankfulness.

WILLIAM SHAKESPEARE

Today I am *Grateful* for: DATE :_____

_____

_____

_____

_____

Today I am *Grateful* for: DATE :_____

_____

_____

_____

_____

Moments that Made Me Smile

DATE :_____

_____

_____

_____

Gratitude, warm, sincere, intense,
when it takes possession of the bosom, fills the soul to overflowing and
scarce leaves room for any other sentiment or thought.

JOHN QUINCY ADAMS

oday I am *Grateful* for: DATE :_____

_____

_____

oday I am *Grateful* for: DATE :_____

_____

_____

oday I am *Grateful* for: DATE :_____

_____

_____

Things I Did for Myself that Made Me Happy

DATE :_____

_____

_____

_____

Gratitude is riches. Complaint is poverty.

D O R I S   D A Y

Today I am *Grateful* for: DATE :_____

_____

_____

_____

_____

Today I am *Grateful* for: DATE :_____

_____

_____

_____

_____

Random Acts of Kindness I Did or Someone Did for Me

DATE :_____

_____

_____

_____

The object of love is to serve, not to win.

WOODROW WILSON

oday I am *Grateful* for:
DATE :_____

_____

_____

oday I am *Grateful* for:
DATE :_____

_____

_____

oday I am *Grateful* for:
DATE :_____

_____

_____

Before Sleep Each Night Ask Yourself,
"What Is the Best Thing That Happened Today?"

DATE :_____

_____

_____

_____

When we give cheerfully and accept gratefully, everyone is blessed.

MAYA ANGELOU

Today I am *Grateful* for:　　　　　DATE :_____

_____

_____

_____

_____

Today I am *Grateful* for:　　　　　DATE :_____

_____

_____

_____

_____

Friends and Family I am Grateful For

DATE :_____

_____

_____

_____

We ought to give thanks for all fortune: if it is good, because it is good, if bad, because it works in us patience, humility and the contempt of this world and the hope of our eternal country.

C.S. LEWIS

Today I am *Grateful* for:

DATE :_____

_____

_____

Today I am *Grateful* for:

DATE :_____

_____

_____

Today I am *Grateful* for:

DATE :_____

_____

_____

Moments that Made Me Smile

DATE :_____

_____

_____

_____

When was the last time you gave thanks because your eyes and and ears were functioning properly?

U N K N O W N

Today I am *Grateful* for: DATE :_____

_____

_____

_____

_____

Today I am *Grateful* for: DATE :_____

_____

_____

_____

_____

Things I Did for Myself that Made Me Happy

DATE :_____

_____

_____

_____

Connecting with those you know love, like and appreciate you restores the spirit and gives you energy to keep moving forward in this life.

DEBORAH DAY

oday I am *Grateful* for: DATE :_____

_____

_____

oday I am *Grateful* for: DATE :_____

_____

_____

oday I am *Grateful* for: DATE :_____

_____

_____

Random Acts of Kindness I Did or Someone Did for Me

DATE :_____

_____

_____

_____

If you're more fortunate than others, build a longer table, not a taller fence.

UNKNOWN

Today I am *Grateful* for: DATE :_____

_____

_____

_____

_____

Today I am *Grateful* for: DATE :_____

_____

_____

_____

_____

Before Sleep Each Night Ask Yourself,
"What Is the Best Thing That Happened Today?"

DATE :_____

_____

_____

_____

Thank you is the best prayer that anyone could say. I say that one a lot. Thank you expresses extreme gratitude, humility, understanding.

ALICE WALKER

Today I am *Grateful* for: DATE :_____

_____

_____

Today I am *Grateful* for: DATE :_____

_____

_____

Today I am *Grateful* for: DATE :_____

_____

_____

Friends and Family I am Grateful For

DATE :_____

_____

_____

_____

You are the best because you brought out the best in us.

Today I am *Grateful* for:
DATE :_____

_____

_____

_____

_____

Today I am *Grateful* for:
DATE :_____

_____

_____

_____

_____

Moments that Made Me Smile

DATE :_____

_____

_____

_____

Now is no time to think of what you do not have.
Think of what you can do with what there is.

ERNEST HEMINGWAY

oday I am *Grateful* for: DATE :_____

_____

_____

oday I am *Grateful* for: DATE :_____

_____

_____

oday I am *Grateful* for: DATE :_____

_____

_____

Things I Did for Myself that Made Me Happy

DATE :_____

_____

_____

_____

God gave you a gift of 84,600 seconds today.
Have you used one of them to say thank you?

WILLIAM ARTHUR WARD

Today I am *Grateful* for: DATE :_____

_____

_____

_____

_____

Today I am *Grateful* for: DATE :_____

_____

_____

_____

_____

Random Acts of Kindness I Did or Someone Did for Me

DATE :_____

_____

_____

_____

*Dwell on the beauty of life. Watch the stars,
and see yourself running with them.*

MARCUS AURELIUS

oday I am *Grateful* for: DATE :_____

_____

_____

oday I am *Grateful* for: DATE :_____

_____

_____

oday I am *Grateful* for: DATE :_____

_____

_____

*Before Sleep Each Night Ask Yourself,
"What Is the Best Thing That Happened Today?"*

DATE :_____

_____

_____

_____

Develop an attitude of gratitude, and give thanks for everything that happens to you, knowing that every step forward is a step toward achieving something bigger and better than your current situation.

BRIAN TRACY

Today I am *Grateful* for: DATE :_____

_____

_____

_____

_____

Today I am *Grateful* for: DATE :_____

_____

_____

_____

_____

Friends and Family I am Grateful For

DATE :_____

_____

_____

_____

Let us remember that, as much has been given us,
uch will be expected from us, and that true homage comes from the heart
as well as from the lips, and shows itself in deeds.

THEODORE ROOSEVELT

oday I am *Grateful* for: DATE :_____

_____

_____

_____

oday I am *Grateful* for: DATE :_____

_____

_____

_____

oday I am *Grateful* for: DATE :_____

_____

_____

_____

Moments that Made Me Smile

DATE :_____

_____

_____

_____

When life is sweet, say thank you and celebrate.
And when life is bitter, say thank you and grow.

SHAUNA NIEQUIST

Today I am *Grateful* for: DATE :_____

_____

_____

_____

_____

Today I am *Grateful* for: DATE :_____

_____

_____

_____

_____

Things I Did for Myself that Made Me Happy

DATE :_____

_____

_____

_____

Blessed are those that can give without remembering
and receive without forgetting.

ELIZABETH BIBESCO

oday I am *Grateful* for: DATE :_____

_____

_____

_____

oday I am *Grateful* for: DATE :_____

_____

_____

_____

oday I am *Grateful* for: DATE :_____

_____

_____

_____

Random Acts of Kindness I Did or Someone Did for Me

DATE :_____

_____

_____

_____

Love your mistake as much as your accomplishments.
Because without mistakes, there wouldn't be any accomplishments.

UNKNOWN

Today I am *Grateful* for: DATE :_____

_____

_____

_____

_____

Today I am *Grateful* for: DATE :_____

_____

_____

_____

_____

Before Sleep Each Night Ask Yourself,
"What Is the Best Thing That Happened Today?"

DATE :_____

_____

_____

_____

I don't have to chase extraordinary moments to find happiness — it's right in front of me if I'm paying attention and practicing gratitude.

BRENE BROWN

Today I am *Grateful* for: DATE :_____

_____

_____

Today I am *Grateful* for: DATE :_____

_____

_____

Today I am *Grateful* for: DATE :_____

_____

_____

Friends and Family I am Grateful For

DATE :_____

_____

_____

_____

The way to develop the best that is in a person is by appreciation and encouragement.

CHARLES SCHWAB

Today I am *Grateful* for: DATE :_____

_____

_____

_____

_____

Today I am *Grateful* for: DATE :_____

_____

_____

_____

_____

Moments that Made Me Smile

DATE :_____

_____

_____

_____

There are always flowers for those who want to see them.

HENRI MATISSE

oday I am *Grateful* for: DATE :_____

_____

_____

oday I am *Grateful* for: DATE :_____

_____

_____

oday I am *Grateful* for: DATE :_____

_____

_____

Things I Did for Myself that Made Me Happy

DATE :_____

_____

_____

_____

Every time you smile at someone,
it is an action of love, a gift to that person, a beautiful thing.

MOTHER TERESA

Today I am *Grateful* for:　　　　　　DATE :_____

_____

_____

_____

_____

Today I am *Grateful* for:　　　　　　DATE :_____

_____

_____

_____

_____

Random Acts of Kindness I Did or Someone Did for Me

DATE :_____

_____

_____

_____

Gratitude; my cup overfloweth.

ANONYMOUS

oday I am *Grateful* for: DATE :_____

_____

_____

oday I am *Grateful* for: DATE :_____

_____

_____

oday I am *Grateful* for: DATE :_____

_____

_____

Before Sleep Each Night Ask Yourself,
"What Is the Best Thing That Happened Today?"

DATE :_____

_____

_____

_____

Yesterday is history. Tomorrow is a mystery. But today is a gift. That's why they call it the present.

VARIOUS, INCLUDING ELEANOR ROOSEVELT

Today I am *Grateful* for: DATE :_____

_____

_____

_____

_____

Today I am *Grateful* for: DATE :_____

_____

_____

_____

_____

Friends and Family I am Grateful For

DATE :_____

_____

_____

_____

Have you ever asked yourself to consciously notice how many things go right in a single day?

PAT WYMAN

oday I am *Grateful* for: DATE :_____

_____

_____

oday I am *Grateful* for: DATE :_____

_____

_____

oday I am *Grateful* for: DATE :_____

_____

_____

Moments that Made Me Smile

DATE :_____

_____

_____

_____

Living in a state of gratitude is the gateway to grace.
ARIANNA HUFFINGTON

Today I am *Grateful* for: DATE :_____

_____

_____

_____

_____

Today I am *Grateful* for: DATE :_____

_____

_____

_____

_____

Things I Did for Myself that Made Me Happy

DATE :_____

_____

_____

_____

Let no one ever come to you without leaving better and happier...

MOTHER TERESA

oday I am *Grateful* for: DATE :_____

_____

_____

oday I am *Grateful* for: DATE :_____

_____

_____

oday I am *Grateful* for: DATE :_____

_____

_____

Random Acts of Kindness I Did or Someone Did for Me

DATE :_____

_____

_____

_____

It's not happiness that brings us gratitude.
It's gratitude that brings us happiness.

ANONYMOUS

Today I am *Grateful* for: DATE :_____

_____

_____

_____

_____

Today I am *Grateful* for: DATE :_____

_____

_____

_____

_____

Before Sleep Each Night Ask Yourself,
"What Is the Best Thing That Happened Today?"

DATE :_____

_____

_____

_____

Reflect upon your present blessings, of which every man has plenty;
not on your past misfortunes, of which all men have some.

CHARLES DICKENS

oday I am *Grateful* for: DATE :_____

_____

_____

oday I am *Grateful* for: DATE :_____

_____

_____

oday I am *Grateful* for: DATE :_____

_____

_____

Friends and Family I am Grateful For

DATE :_____

_____

_____

_____

Be thankful when you don't know something
For it gives you the opportunity to learn.

ANONYMOUS

Today I am *Grateful* for: DATE :_____

_____

_____

_____

_____

Today I am *Grateful* for: DATE :_____

_____

_____

_____

_____

Moments that Made Me Smile

DATE :_____

_____

_____

_____

Piglet noticed that even though he had a very small heart,
it could hold a rather large amount of gratitude.

A.A. MILNE, WINNIE-THE-POOH

oday I am *Grateful* for: DATE :_____

_____

_____

oday I am *Grateful* for: DATE :_____

_____

_____

oday I am *Grateful* for: DATE :_____

_____

_____

Things I Did for Myself that Made Me Happy

DATE :_____

_____

_____

_____

True forgiveness is when you can say, "Thank you for that experience".
OPRAH WINFREY

Today I am *Grateful* for: DATE :_____

_____

_____

_____

_____

Today I am *Grateful* for: DATE :_____

_____

_____

_____

_____

Random Acts of Kindness I Did or Someone Did for Me

DATE :_____

_____

_____

_____

Every single day find at least one thing to be grateful for.

ANONYMOUS

oday I am *Grateful* for: DATE :_____

_____

_____

oday I am *Grateful* for: DATE :_____

_____

_____

oday I am *Grateful* for: DATE :_____

_____

_____

Before Sleep Each Night Ask Yourself,
"What Is the Best Thing That Happened Today?"

DATE :_____

_____

_____

_____

At times our own light goes out and is rekindled by a spark from another person. Each of us has cause to think with deep gratitude of those who have lighted the flame within us.

ALBERT SCHWEITZER

Today I am *Grateful* for:　　　　　　　　DATE :_____

_____

_____

_____

_____

Today I am *Grateful* for:　　　　　　　　DATE :_____

_____

_____

_____

_____

Friends and Family I am Grateful For

DATE :_____

_____

_____

_____

You simply will not be the same person two months from now after consciously giving thanks each day for the abundance that exists in your life. And you will have set in motion an ancient spiritual law: the more you have and are grateful for, the more will be given you.

SARAH BAN BREATHNACH

Today I am *Grateful* for:

DATE :_____

_____

_____

Today I am *Grateful* for:

DATE :_____

_____

_____

Today I am *Grateful* for:

DATE :_____

_____

_____

Moments that Made Me Smile

DATE :_____

_____

_____

_____

It isn't what you have in your pocket that makes you thankful, but what you have in your heart.

AUTHOR UNKNOWN

Today I am *Grateful* for:　　　　　　　　DATE :＿＿＿＿＿＿＿＿

_____

_____

_____

_____

Today I am *Grateful* for:　　　　　　　　DATE :＿＿＿＿＿＿＿＿

_____

_____

_____

_____

Things I Did for Myself that Made Me Happy

DATE :＿＿＿＿＿＿＿＿

_____

_____

_____

Gratitude is multiplied when you think of it as your new view of the world.

PAT WYMAN

Today I am *Grateful* for: DATE :_____

_____

_____

Today I am *Grateful* for: DATE :_____

_____

_____

Today I am *Grateful* for: DATE :_____

_____

_____

Random Acts of Kindness I Did or Someone Did for Me

DATE :_____

_____

_____

_____

Goodnight stars, goodnight air, goodnight noises everywhere.

FROM GOODNIGHT MOON BY MARGARET WISE BROWN

Today I am *Grateful* for: DATE :_____

_____

_____

_____

_____

Today I am *Grateful* for: DATE :_____

_____

_____

_____

_____

Before Sleep Each Night Ask Yourself,
"What Is the Best Thing That Happened Today?"

DATE :_____

_____

_____

_____

Among the things you can give and still keep are your word, a smile, and a grateful heart.

ZIG ZIGLAR

oday I am *Grateful* for: DATE :_____

_____

_____

oday I am *Grateful* for: DATE :_____

_____

_____

oday I am *Grateful* for: DATE :_____

_____

_____

Friends and Family I am Grateful For

DATE :_____

_____

_____

_____

Thankfulness creates gratitude which generates contentment that causes peace.

TODD STOCKER

Today I am *Grateful* for: DATE :_____

_____

_____

_____

_____

Today I am *Grateful* for: DATE :_____

_____

_____

_____

_____

Moments that Made Me Smile

DATE :_____

_____

_____

_____

I've never before been so aware of the thousands of little good things, the thousands of things that go right every day.

A.J. JACOBS

oday I am *Grateful* for: DATE :_____

_____

_____

oday I am *Grateful* for: DATE :_____

_____

_____

oday I am *Grateful* for: DATE :_____

_____

_____

Things I Did for Myself that Made Me Happy

DATE :_____

_____

_____

_____

Try leaving a trail of little sparks of gratitude on your daily trips. You will be surprised how they will set small flames of friendship that will be rose beacons on your next visit.

DALE CARNEGIE

Today I am *Grateful* for: DATE :_____

_____

_____

_____

_____

Today I am *Grateful* for: DATE :_____

_____

_____

_____

_____

Random Acts of Kindness I Did or Someone Did for Me

DATE :_____

_____

_____

_____

The power of finding beauty in the humblest things makes the home happy and life lovely.

LOUISA MAY ALCOTT

oday I am *Grateful* for: DATE :_____

_____

_____

oday I am *Grateful* for: DATE :_____

_____

_____

oday I am *Grateful* for: DATE :_____

_____

_____

Before Sleep Each Night Ask Yourself,
"What Is the Best Thing That Happened Today?"

DATE :_____

_____

_____

_____

Even the smallest blessing on earth is enough reason to be thankful for your life.

E D M O N D   M B I A K A

Today I am *Grateful* for: DATE :_____

_____

_____

_____

_____

Today I am *Grateful* for: DATE :_____

_____

_____

_____

_____

Friends and Family I am Grateful For

DATE :_____

_____

_____

_____

Gratitude bestows reverence, allowing us to encounter every day epiphanies, those transcendent moments of awe that change forever how we experience life and the world.

SARAH BAN BREATHNACH

ɔday I am *Grateful* for: DATE :_____

_____

_____

ɔday I am *Grateful* for: DATE :_____

_____

_____

ɔday I am *Grateful* for: DATE :_____

_____

_____

Moments that Made Me Smile

DATE :_____

_____

_____

_____

Our greatest joys in life are determined by what we do with our gratitude. This is the secret to living a joy—filled life: Finding the smallest reason to be thankful and letting it wash over your heart and change your perspective forever

ASHLEY REALE

Today I am *Grateful* for: DATE :_____

_____

_____

_____

_____

Today I am *Grateful* for: DATE :_____

_____

_____

_____

_____

Things I Did for Myself that Made Me Happy

DATE :_____

_____

_____

_____

As her head rests on her pillow, she'll go through the alphabet from A to Z and try to think of something to be grateful for that starts with each letter...

A.J. JACOBS

oday I am *Grateful* for: DATE :_____

_____

_____

oday I am *Grateful* for: DATE :_____

_____

_____

oday I am *Grateful* for: DATE :_____

_____

_____

Random Acts of Kindness I Did or Someone Did for Me

DATE :_____

_____

_____

_____

We hope you love this journal as much as we loved creating it for you.
What changed or got better in your life now that you have completed the journa

---

SHARE YOUR GRATITUDE WITH US!

We'd love to hear from you! Share your biggest insights and let us know how
journaling in The One-Minute Gratitude Journal has made your life better.
We will share this in future books - just with your first name of course!

✉ **Email: oneminutejournals@gmail.com**

Want to give The One-Minute Gratitude Journal as a gift to your friends,
family or to show appreciation for those in your workplace or at school?

Here is the link: https://amzn.to/2UUFJh7
For bulk discounts: **oneminutejournals@gmail.com**

Freebies for You!

1. FREE Gratitude Course
2. FREE videos on how gratitude changes lives
3. Scientific benefits of gratitude and surprise freebies

VISIT OUR WEBSITE

https://www.HowtoLearn.com/Free-Gratitude-Course

Made in the USA
Middletown, DE
21 January 2023